Charles George Vernon Harcourt

Legends of St. Augustine, St. Anthony, and St. Cuthbert

Charles George Vernon Harcourt

Legends of St. Augustine, St. Anthony, and St. Cuthbert

ISBN/EAN: 9783741158193

Manufactured in Europe, USA, Canada, Australia, Japa

Cover: Foto ©Thomas Meinert / pixelio.de

Manufactured and distributed by brebook publishing software
(www.brebook.com)

Charles George Vernon Harcourt

Legends of St. Augustine, St. Anthony, and St. Cuthbert

LEGENDS

OF

ST. AUGUSTINE, ST. ANTHONY,

AND

ST. CUTHBERT,

PAINTED

ON THE BACK OF THE STALLS IN CARLISLE CATHEDRAL.

CARLISLE:
PRINTED AT THE OFFICES OF C. THURNAM AND SONS.
1868.

PREFACE.

The Legends painted on the back of the Stalls were, till the late restoration of the Cathedral, supposed, on Todd's authority, to be due to the care of Prior Senhouse, under whose directions the ceiling in the Deanery was painted. In Todd's M.S. the authority for his statement is generally noted in the margin; but in this instance none having been assigned, it occurred to me that as there appeared to be no external authority, there must be some internal one for Todd's statement. Accordingly I requested Mr. Purday to examine the paintings, to see if he could discover any date. He did so, and found on one of the panels, where the devil is represented in company with St. Augustine, Prior Gondibour's initials,  (T. P. G.) stencilled all over it. These initials are also to be found carved on wood in St. Catherine's Chapel, and on stone in the North Aisle, and in the Crypt under the Fratry. The paintings of St. Augustine and St. Cuthbert, if they ever were whitewashed, had been uncovered before Todd's time. The others of St. Anthony and the Apostles were brought to light by Dean Percy; but they have remained hitherto but ill deciphered in several instances, and unexplained.

I have been enabled to make out the meaning of the greatest part, but there are still some portions on which I can at present throw no light.

For instance, though I have had the advantage of consulting Lives of the Saints kindly lent me by Mr. Howard, of Corby, as well as the books in the Chapter Library, I do not find anything about the woman who saw St. Augustine during his meditation on the Trinity; nor can I discover any notice of the three men he sent somewhere to be healed.

Two of these Legends, St. Augustine and St. Anthony, were copied in the year 1795, by Thomas Carlyle, a Carlisle artist. The copies are in the possession of Mr. Wm. Forster, who thinks it probable that they were ordered by the Rev. Mr. Boucher, the well-known antiquarian, a native of Blencogo, who took up his residence in Carlisle a few years after these copies were made, but before this was occupied in the formation of a Glossary of Provincial Terms, and would naturally therefore take an interest in these Legends. Copies have also been made by Mr. Nutter, and from one of them, which Mr. Cowen was so good as to lend Lady Frances Harcourt, she made copies, which, having been submitted to the anastatical process, she has given to me to publish. Lady Frances, however, had already copied the Legend of St. Cuthbert, which had not before been copied from the original. In the Legend of St. Augustine, in the engraving No. 6, the words proceeding out of his mouth, "*In inferna demergimur*," has been accidentally omitted. The words are correctly given in the short explanatory notices I have appended.

C. G. V. HARCOURT.

1

Here fader and modr of Sanct Austine
First put hym here to lerne doctrine

Here taught he gramor and rethorike
Amongys all doctors non was hy lyke.

Her promysid he wt hys moder to abide
Bot he left hr wepyng t Italy e tyde

Thus taught he at rome the seuyn science
yt was gret price tyll hys presence

Her prechyd Ambrose and oft tymes prevyd
Adlita accid wych Austine mevid

Her poinciane hym tald ye lyfe of Sanct Anton
And to Elypias he stoyshed said thus onone

Ver sore wepyng for hys gret syn
He went to morne a garth wyth in

Her wepynge and walyng as he lay
Sodenly a voice thus herde he say

9

No word for to to warke her myght he say
But wrate to the pepil For hym to pray

Her of sanct Ambrose chrystenyd was
The gret Doctor Austyne throgh Godys grace.

11

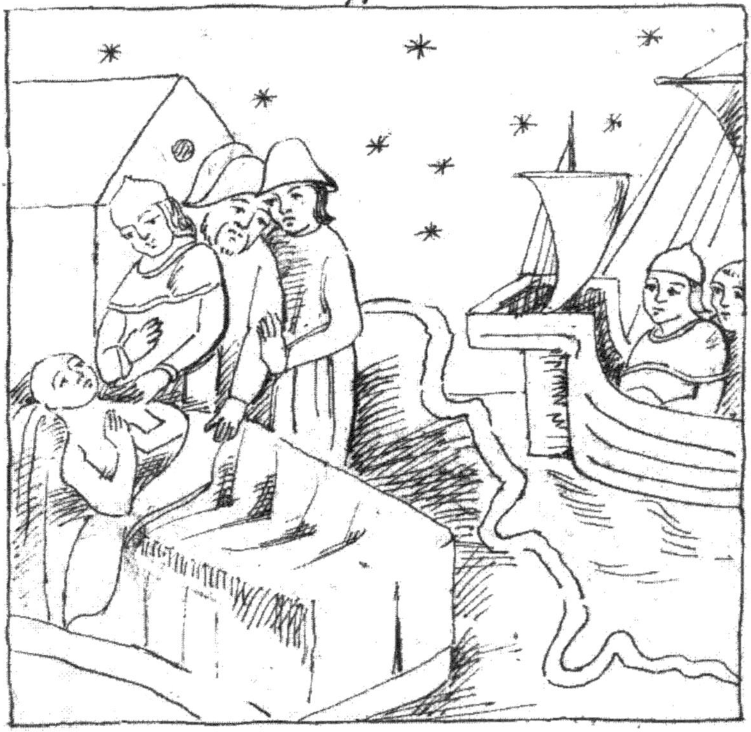

Her deyd hys moder called monica
As þai wer returnyng to Affrica

12

Her was he sacred prest and alyd
Of Valery the byshop thoffe he refusyd

Her after ……………
Hys …… of religion as ye may sea

Her Fortunate the heretyk condemnit be
Informing the lawyes of maniche

Consecrate byshop was thys doctour
By all the cuntre with gret honour.

Any woman come to hi for consolacion
She saw hym wt the trinite in meditacion

When he compleyn had sayd & come to luke
He was full clere out of ye knavys buke

Thay beried hys body with all diligence
Hexam hys awyn kyrk of þ ponence

Thay beried hys body with all diligence
Here in hys awyn kyrk of yponence

19

Her Liedprand the King of Lumberdy
hym translate frō Sardyne to Pauye

Thei shrynyd hys banes solemnly
In Sanct Peters kyrk thar at Pavye

Thys priorle bad soon do ekyn lang her
And helyd hym that was his thre yer

Her he apperyd unto thes men thre
And bad yam go to .... yt hole

LEGEND OF ST. AUGUSTINE.

No. 1.

St. Augustine was born in 367, in the 10th year of the reign of Constantius Constantine, at Tagaste, a town in Numidia. The rod in the schoolmaster's hand perhaps signifies St. Augustine's dislike to the rudiments of learning, reading, writing, and arithmetic. Indeed, according to the account he gives of himself in his Confessions, he seems to have been a very naughty boy. From Tagaste he went to Madurus, because the liberal Arts were taught in that city.

Her Fader and Mod[r] of Sanct Austyne
Fyrst put him her to lerne doctrine.

No. 2.

When he was nineteen years of age he taught rhetoric at Carthage, and from thence he went to Rome, in the 28th year of his age.

Her taught he gramor and rethoricke;
Emongys all doctors non was h' lyke.

No. 3.

He went to Rome not so much because his salary and dignity would be greater, but because the scholars there were quieter and better behaved. His mother, Monica, complained bitterly of his intentions to do so, and wanted either to prevent his going, or to go with him. She followed him to the sea shore, and he persuaded her to remain for the night in a place dedicated to St. Cyprian, near the ship.* But the wind was fair, and he succeeded in escaping while she was praying that he might be prevented from sailing; and the next morning she filled the air with her cries.

> Her promysed w[t] his moder to abide,
> Bot he left h[r] weping and stal the tyde.
>
> On the sail of the ship, "Grace de diu."

No. 4.

He taught rhetoric at Rome, but was deserted by some of his pupils, and went to Milan, to teach rhetoric there, having been selected for that purpose by the Prefect of Rome, who had been asked by the Milanese to choose them a Professor.

> There taught he at Rome the sevyn science;
> Y[r] was gret prece tyll his presence.

No. 5.

He had an introduction to Ambrose, the Archbishop, and went to hear his sermons, partly to ascertain whether he was as eloquent as he was said to be. Though he went to hear the manner, he at last reflected on the matter. He found that many of the doctrines of the Manichœans were false, and many of the objections against the Scriptures doubtful, and he determined to become a catechumen in the Catholic Church, which had been recommended to him by his parents. He rejoiced that he no longer read the books of the law and Prophets with that irreverent feeling

* She used, according to the African custom, to bring offerings to the monuments of the saints, from which custom St. Ambrose afterwards dissuaded her.

which he had formerly entertained, thinking they propounded absurdities, and mistaking their real meaning. He gladly heard Ambrose preaching that "The letter killeth, but the Spirit giveth life." *Litera occidit, Spiritus autem vivificat.* Ambrose, removing the veil of mystery, showed how the letter must be spiritually explained.

> Her prechyd Ambrose and oft tymes previd
> Q^{d} l^{tra} occid^{t} wych Austyne mevid.

No. 6.

Alypius, his countryman, had gone to learn law at Rome, where Augustine found him. He accompanied Augustine to Milan. They happened to be together alone, and there was a gaming table before them with the Epistles of St. Paul upon it, which Augustine was studying at that time. A military officer, who was a Christian, came to visit Augustine, took the book up, and joking with Augustine about his Christian studies, related to him the life of St. Anthony, and also how two of his companions, who accidentally met with it, had become monks and their wives nuns. Augustine, much disturbed by Politianus's story, went to Alypius, and exclaimed—"*Quid patimur? Quid est hoc? Surgunt indocti et Cœlum rapiunt, et nos cum doctrinis nostris sine corde; ecce volutamur in carne et sanguine!*" [What do we suffer? What is this? The unlearned arise and take Heaven by storm, and we with our learning without a heart; see where we wallow in flesh and blood.] In the legend, "*In inferna,*" or "*in infera demergimur,*" is substituted for the last sentence—"We are sunk into the lowest places," or "into the pit of hell." His friend was astonished, for his forehead, his cheeks, his eyes, the tone of his voice, spoke more than his words.

> Her poinciane hym tald ye lyffe of Sanct Anton,
> And to Elipius he said thus anon,
> Q^{d} patim^{r} surgu'^{t} indocti et Cœlu' rapiu't
> Et nos cu' doctrinis i' infer^{r} demergimur.

No. 7.

He went into a garden to be alone; he tore his hair, beat his forehead, and embraced his knees with his closed fingers. Alypius followed him.

> Her sore wepyng for hys gret syn,
> He went to morne a garth wythin.

No. 8.

He burst, at length, into a flood of tears, and went to weep by himself under a fig tree, and cried out—"How long wilt thou be angry with me? for ever? How long—to-morrow and to-morrow? Why not now? why not in this hour the end of my baseness? And lo! I hear a voice, as it were of a boy or a girl, singing and frequently repeating, '*Tolle lege, Tolle lege.*'" He thought this was a divine order to him to read the book (the Epistles of St. Paul) which he had left with Alypius. Remembering how St. Anthony had considered the words, "Sell all thou hast," addressed to himself, he seized and opened the book and read the first words which presented themselves (Romans xiii, 13), "*Not in revelling and drunkenness, not in chambering and wantonness, not in strife and envying; but put ye on the Lord Jesus Christ, and make not provision for the flesh, to fulfil the lusts thereof.*" He read no more ; the darkness of doubt was changed into the light of security. Alypius, to whom he showed the passage, reading on, met with the words immediately following—"*Receive him that is weak in the faith.*" His morals had been purer than St. Augustine's, whom he had dissuaded from marriage ; and he too was converted forthwith.

Her wepyng and walyng as he lay,
Sodenly a voice thus herd he say,
Tolle lege, Tolle lege.

No. 9.

He had the toothache, so that he could not speak, and he bethought himself he might write on wax and ask those around to pray for him. No sooner had he knelt down to pray than the pain vanished.

No worde for tothewarke here myght he say,
But wrote to the pepel for him to pray.

No. 10.

Alypius and his son were baptized with him, and the words of the *Te Deum, Te Deum laudamus, Te Dominum confitemur*, are put into his mouth, because, according to one account, he composed it, and according to another, Ambrose and he composed it between them, reciting alternate verses extempore.

Her of Sainct Ambrose chrysteyned was
The gret doctor Austyne thogh Godes grace.
Te Deum laudamus, Te Dom' confitemur.

No. 11.

Among others, Simplicianus made demonstration of exceeding joy, and besought Augustine to give him some manner of rules in writing. For although all the religious men of his monastery agreed together in the service of God, yet they did it not by rule, but as every one liked ; this man fasted, another prayed, another used discipline. St. Augustine then came into the deserts of Tuscany, which he calleth Mons Pisanus, and there he gave a second rule. Hearing that there dwelt certain religious men, living like hermits, he visited them, and remained with them one whole year. After these things, being entreated by his mother to return to Africa, he departed with her to Ostia, where she died. Her two sons, Augustine and Navigius, who may be seen in the picture, being present.

Her deyd his moder, called Monica,
As thai were returning to Affrica.

No. 12.

St. Valerius, Bishop of Hippo, heard great fame of St. Augustine, and was thereof being glad, hoping he might be to him a great help in the government of his Church. The good Bishop endeavoured to get St. Augustine unto him ; but he excused himself, and kept himself away, lest he might be chosen bishop by force. Valerius was much pleased to see the heavenly life St. Augustine and his religious men led. In order to reprove one of those who had gone to Hippo to revenge his father's murder, St. Augustine followed him ; and Valerius hearing of his arrival, told the people he wanted a curate. The people entreated St. Augustine to take the office. They surrounded him, and conducted him to Valerius, who in a manner by compulsion ordered him and made him Priest. St. Augustine drew back and excused himself, but the Bishop would admit of no excuse. Possedonius says that when St. Augustine was asked why he received the dignity so unwillingly, he answered—"Because the place of Priest is near that of Bishop." St. Valerius gave St. Augustine a garden outside the city to build a monastery on. This was the second convent of his order; and he wrote the rule now observed by the religious men.

Her was he sacred prest and usyd
Of Valery the Bishop thoffe he refusyt.

No. 13.

This picture must refer to St. Augustine giving his third rule in Africa.

Her after [virtue's law instructed he]
Hys [men of] religion as ye may see.

No. 14.

He disputed with Fortunatus, maintaining that the evil in man proceeded from his own free will. Fortunatus contended that evil was co-eternal with the Deity. Fortunatus had been successful in making perverts to Manichœism. The day after this dispute he acknowledged he had nothing to say for himself, and left Hippo.

Her Fortunate the Heretyk concludit he,
Informing the laws of Maneche.

No. 15.

Valerius was not satisfied till he had got certain Bishops to consecrate St. Augustine, who had begun to preach. He made him his coadjutor.

St. Augustine was now 37; and he assembled the clergy in the Bishop's house, and gave them a rule then how they should live without property, and that they should promise to observe the three ordinary vows of religious men.

> Consecrate Byshop was this doctour
> By all the cuntre with gret honour.

No. 16.

This picture must refer to the time when Augustine composed his book, "De Trinitate." Properly speaking, there is no woman connected with the story.

Augustine, after his baptism, would never speak to any woman in private, if he could help it. While composing the treatise on the Trinity, he had a vision of a child making a little pit, and St. Augustine demanding what he would do, he answered that he would put into that little pit all the water in the sea. The simple childish answer made the holy doctor smile, telling the child that it was a thing impossible. The child replied—"Thou thinkest this a difficult matter; but I tell thee, the enterprise which thou hast undertaken, thinking with thy weak understanding to penetrate the high mystery of the blessed Trinity, is much more difficult." The child having said this, vanished. Whereby St. Augustine understood that he was sent by God to advertise him of his bold attempt, and so he stayed his hand to write any more of that matter, and was diligent to amend and correct that which he had written.

> As this woman come to hym for consolacion
> She saw hym wth ye trinite in meditacion.

No. 17.

Complyn is the last service in the Romish Liturgy. So when he had performed the last service, the Devil was disappointed in finding that he was clean out of his book, in which he supposed him to be, and was sorry that he showed it him.

When he Complyn had sayd and come to luke,
He was full clene out of the knafy's buke.

Pœnitet me tibi ostendisse librum.

No. 18.

In the year of our Lord 433, the Vandals, being driven out of Spain, passed into Africa, and besieged Hippo. Augustine died during the siege, and was buried "*in Ecclesiâ suâ Hipponensi.*"

The barbarians took the city after his death, and his body was carried into Sardinia.

They beried his body with diligence
Her in hys auyn kyrk of Yp'onense.

No. 19.

Afterwards, Luitbrand, king of Lombardy, bought this blessed body of the Saracens, and buried it honourably at Pavia.

Her Liedbrand, the kyng of Lumberdy,
Hym translate fro' Sardyne to Pavye.

No. 20.

Thei shryned his banes solmenly
In St. Peter's Kyrk thus at Pavye.

No. 21.

St. Augustine, after he went to Africa, healed by his prayers the leg of Innocentius, who lodged with him. Perhaps this picture refers to this.

This Prior he bad soon do Evynsang her
And helyd hym that was sek thre yer.

No. 22.

He blesses and heals several lame persons.

Her be apperyd unto these men thre
And bad yam go to............yt hale.

Of Anton story who lyke to here.
In Egypt was he born and boyth hys fere

. Her is be baptyd Anton ther hym sall
gret landes and rentten to hym weth fall

Fro scole to the kyrke her in be gayn
To here the sermoun that afyre be in tayn

4

Here geveth he the kyrk both land and rent
To leve in povert in hys intent

Here in Agello to oon an old man he went
To lerne perfeccion in hys intent

Here makyth he breder an urn of religō
And techyth them virtule in p̄ feccō

Here to the wyldernes an ermet gon he
& than temptyth hym covetyce with oon gold dyshe

8

The spryt of Fornicacōn to hỹ doth her apper
& thenne he chasteth hys body with thorne & brer

Þe devill þat hym wounded wᵗʰ lance and staf
And levyt hym for deyd lyyng at hys cave

Her Crist harth hȳ helyd the devill he dot away
& comfortyd hym confessor deyd ar he lay

Here comandrte ye bestn and ffalt alway ye flre
Ye bore hy obbayn and ws hy byden he

Here makyth he a well and water hath uptayne
And comfortyd hyr breder thyrst was nere slayne

Here comãndeth þe best to mak hȳ a cave
& þen þe berys Paulyn & lay hȳ in grave

Than walked he over ye Flode water doth hym dere
Theodor hȳ left dar not cū hȳ rere.

15 16

Here departith Anton to hevyn hys saule is gone
Beried ther hym his breder in wildernes alone

Her in wildernes yt bery hym ij women And hys knawls
For God he comanded hym home first ya draw

17

Thus levyth he ĩ wildernes xxt yere & more
Withoutany company bot the wyld bore.

LEGEND OF ST. ANTHONY.

No. 1.

St. Anthony was born in a village in Egypt, A.D. 251, called by Butler, in the Lives of the Saints, "*Coma.*" This may probably be a mistake, similar to one which occurs in the Legend. Only here the Greek word for village, "*Coma,*" seems turned into a proper name. In the legend of the paintings the Latin word "*Agello,*" a various translation, instead of "*Pago,*" taken from the version of Evagrius, is treated in the same way.

Of Anton's story who lyste to here
In Egypt was he bornt as doyth aper.

No. 2.

His parents were Christians, and had an independent fortune, which fell to him by their death, at the age of nineteen.

Her is he bapty'd Anton they him call
Gret landes and renttes to hym doth fawl.

No. 3.

Nearly six months afterwards he was reflecting, as he walked to Church, how the Apostles, leaving everything, had followed their Master; and how those mentioned in the Acts had sold their goods and placed the price at the feet of the Apostles, that it might be given to the poor, and what was laid up for them in heaven. He entered the Church and heard these words of the Gospel read—"If thou wilt be perfect, go sell all that thou hast, and give it to the poor, and *come and follow me, and then thou shalt have treasure in heaven.*"

As scoler to the kyrk is he gayn
To hear the sermontt and afyre he has tayn.

No. 4.

Considering these words as addressed to himself, he immediately, as if by a divine impulse, left the Church and delivered up his paternal estate (120 acres of good land) to the people of the village, that they might never trouble him or his sister; and selling his moveables, gave the price of them, which was considerable, to the poor. He first kept something for his young sister; but going again to Church, and hearing the words—"*Take no thought for the morrow,*' he, without further delay, distributed even that to the poor, and placed his sister in a convent.

Her geyffith he to the kyrke both land and rent,
To leve in povert is his intent.

No. 5.

He went to an old man who lived in a neighbouring village to learn perfection. At that time there were few monasteries, and none in distant deserts. The ascetics lived near their own villages alone.

St. Anthony besides sought to attain perfection by going wherever he heard of eminent saints, and imitating their virtues.

Her in Agello* to oon auld man he went,
To lerne perfeccion is hys intent.

---

* Agello means small field.

No. 6.

All pious people admired him, called him a friend of God, and saluted him as a son or brother. But his excitement (20 years after this) to found monasteries, his exhortations to the monks, and his government of these institutions, is no doubt referred to here, though it happened after his temptations, when his brethren, after he had lived in the strictest seclusion for twenty years, almost forcibly induced him to come out.

St Anthony says to the monks to whom he gave a lecture—"*The dæmons attack Christians and monks, especially when they see them making religious proselytes, as I know by experience. They suggest wicked thoughts, but are overthrown by prayers and fasting, and faith in the Lord. But one overthrow does not satisfy them; if they cannot catch your heart with obscene pleasure, they will take another way, and try to terrify you by various visions, putting on the form of a woman, of beasts, serpents, and giants, and of bands of soldiers; but you need not be afraid; for with the aid of faith and the sign of the cross they suddenly vanish away. They make much noise and raise up a great tumult, but they are very timid. They sometimes appear in the shape of Leviathan, with flames coming out of their mouths, sometimes like monks singing Psalms, quoting Scripture, and giving good advice. When the devils appeared with a light, he shut his eyes; when they clapped, and hissed, and danced, he prayed and sang Psalms; when a very tall one came, calling himself the Power and Providence of God, and offered him anything he pleased, he spit upon him and tried to strike him, and thought he succeeded. He called on the name of Christ, and immediately he vanished, with all his fellow dæmons.*"

Here makyth he breder as men of relig'
And techyth them virtu to leve in perfecco'

No. 7.

In the 37th year of his age he wanted the old man to go with him to a desert mountain. Upon his refusal, he went alone. The Devil threw the phantasy of a great silver dish in his way. Anthony guessed at the fraud, and discovering the Devil in it, reproached him thus— "There is no beaten path, no footstep of travellers; this could not, from its size, have fallen out of anyone's vest. If it had been lost, the loser might easily have returned and found it, as it is in such a desert place. This is the Devil's art! O Devil! thou shalt not prevail. Avaunt! May this go with you to damnation!" And when he had said this the dish vanished into smoke. Going thence he found not a phantasy, but true gold in the way. But St. Athanasius doubts whether an angel or devil put it there. It might be an angel, to prove to the Devil that St. Anthony did not care about money.

Her to the wyldernes as armet [hermit] geon he,
And thus temptyth hym covytice with one gold dyshie.

No. 8.

The Devil [or Spirit of Fornication] appeared to him in the beginning of his temptations, having first, however, suggested such things as these:—The memory of his possessions, the care of his sister, his relations, the value of money, the love of glory, the various pleasures of luxury, the laboriousness of virtue. He set against all these the love of Christ and the torments of hell. He chastened his body with want of food and sleep, and with lying on the cold ground; but *not* with briars, at least St. Athanasius does not say so. The Devil afterwards appeared to him in the shape of a black boy, and told him he was the Spirit of Fornication.

> The Spyritt of Fornicacion to hy' her doth apper,
> & thus he chastith his body with thorn & brer [briars].

No. 9.

In quest of a more remote solitude, he withdrew further from his village, and hid himself in an old sepulchre, whither a friend brought him from time to time a little bread. Satan, fearing lest the desert should soon be filled with ascetics, came with a host of devils, and one night beat him till he lay for dead on the ground. This caused him excessive pain. In this state his friend found him, and took him to the village church, and his relations and friends thought he was dead. But coming to himself, at night he told his friend to tell nobody, but carry him back to the cave. He was not able to stand; but as he lay he defied the devils in the name of Christ. Upon this Satan entered with his devils and returned to the charge, and having split the walls of the cave with this noise, and put on the shape of all sorts of beasts and reptiles, threatening him; but he said—"If you had any strength one of you would have been enough. You try to terrify me with your numbers, but it is a proof of your imbecility that you put on the shape of brute beasts."

> The devill thus hath hy' wounded with lance and staf
> And levyth hy' for deyd lyying at his cayf [cave].

No. 10.

At last a ray of heavenly light broke in upon him; his pain was relieved, and the dæmons vanished. Anthony addressed the vision, and said—"Where wert thou? why didst thou not appear at first to put an end to my trouble?" A voice answered—"Anthony, I was here; I waited to behold thy conflict; as thou enduredst and wast not worsted, I will always be your helper, and will make you everywhere famous." Anthony rose and prayed, and seemed to himself stronger than ever.

Her Crist haith hym helyd the devill he dot away
& comfortyd his confessor deyd as he lay.

No. 11.

He always fasted, and had an under garment of sackcloth and an outer one of skin. He never washed his body nor his feet, unless he was obliged to walk in the water. Nobody ever saw him undressed till he was buried. He was afraid his parents would think too highly of him in consequence of his miraculous cures, or that he might be puffed up himself. As he was going to the upper Thebais to visit persons to whom he was unknown, he was waiting for a ship by the side of the river, when a Divine voice enjoined him to go to a place in the wilderness, on a high mountain, distant three days journey. His brethren brought him bread; but that he might not fatigue them, he asked them to bring him a spade, and a pickaxe, and a little corn. He then selected a little spot, well watered, and fit for a garden. In this he cultivated what he wanted for bread; but as he still had visitors, he planted some potherbs for their refreshment. At first the wild animals came for the purpose of drinking, and often injured his vegetables; but he graciously laying hold of one of them, said to all—"Why do you injure *me*, who never injured *you?* Go away in the name of the Lord; never come near me again." And from that time, as if afraid of his injunction, they never came near the place. The dæmons, however, sent beasts of prey and hyænas against him; but when they threatened to eat him up, he said—"If you have any power given you, eat me up forthwith; but if you are suborned by dæmons, depart! for I am the servant of Christ." The beasts, as if chased away by that word, immediately fled. Afterwards, however, there came a beast with a human figure above, with the legs and feet of an ass. Anthony, signing himself with the cross, said—"I am the servant of Christ; if you are sent against me, here I am." The beast fled away with the dæmons, but in such haste that he fell down and was killed. This was the ruin of the dæmons.

Her com'ands he y^{is} bests and ffast away they flie
Y^{e} bore hy' obbays and wth hy' bided he.

No. 12.

Being asked by some monks to come down and visit them, he went with them, and they carried bread and water on a camel. There was no water, except on the mountain where his monastery was; so on the journey they were nearly dying of thirst, and had dismissed their camel in despair. Anthony prayed for them, and a spring of water burst forth; and they got their camel again, which had been detained by a providential accident.

Her makyth he a well and water hath uptayne
And comforted hys breder thyrst was nere slaine.

No. 13.

Anthony was inclined to think himself the chief of hermits, and it was revealed to him in a dream that there was another monk better than himself, in another solitude, and that he ought to go and visit him. This was the blessed Paul, who was 113 years old, St. Anthony at this time being near 90. He set out, not knowing which way to turn. He first met a centaur; and whether it was sent by the Devil to frighten him, or whether it was a natural product of the desert, which often produces monsters, St. Jerome doubts. However, it told Anthony the way. He then met a satyr, who asked him to pray for him and his race. He was ultimately guided to the cave where Paul lived by a wolf; but as he was cautiously feeling his way, he stumbled, and Paul immediately hearing the noise, shut the door and bolted it. After St. Anthony had entreated him for six hours, Paul let him in. A crow, which used to supply the latter with half a loaf, on this occasion brought a whole one. Paul then told Anthony he was about to die, and Anthony was divinely sent to bury him; he wished, therefore, he would wrap him up in a cloak (which had been given to Anthony by Athanasius), and that he would go immediately and fetch it,—not that he wanted it, but that he wished to spare Anthony the pain of seeing him die. Anthony was much astonished that Paul should know that there was such a cloak; but he went for it, and on his return saw Paul's scul carried up to heaven amidst a host of angels, prophets, and apostles. He flew forwards to look for him, and found him on his knees, with his hands lifted up in the attitude of prayer, and knelt to pray with him; but observing he did not, as usual, sigh during his prayer, rushed to him with a tearful embrace, and discovered that it was a corpse which was praying! He had no spade to dig a grave, and wished to stay to die by his side, when two lions with flowing manes suddenly appeared. Anthony, trusting in God, awaited them as if they had been doves. They came straight up to the corpse, and wagging their tails and fawning upon it, lay down at its feet. Then they wanted to show their grief. They presently began to scratch the ground, and made a hole large enough for a grave; and immediately holding back their necks and moving their ears, they signified that they wanted payment, and coming up to Anthony, licked his hands and feet. He saw that they wished him to bless them, so he granted their wish and ordered them to go away. He buried Paul and took his tunic, made of palm leaves, which he always wore at Easter and Whitsuntide.

Her commandith he best to mak hy' a cayf
& thus he berys Paulyn & lay hy' in graf.

No. 14.

The story about the water is evidently transferred from Ammas to Anthony. Athanasius relates it thus:—Ammas had to cross the river Lycus during a flood. He desired Theodore, who was with him, to go to a distance, that they might not see one another naked as they swam through the water. Then when Theodore departed, he was so ashamed to see himself naked, and whilst he was blushing and reflected, he was suddenly carried across. Theodore, when he returned, was astonished to see he had got over without being wet. He lays hold of Ammas's feet, and says he will not let him go till he tells him how this happened. Ammas tells him he did not walk on the water (but this could only be done by Divine permission)—that he was carried over, but that he must tell nobody this before his death.

Thus walked he over the flode water doth hy' no der [harm]
Theodor hy' se and dar not cu' hy' nere.

No. 15.

Anthony saw Ammas carried up to heaven, and a number of angels meeting him and congratulating him. He was told by a voice that it was Ammas, and afterwards found that he had died at that time. St. Jerome says that he saw Paul carried up to heaven; but I do not find any old account of his own translation having been seen.

Her departith Anton to hevyn his saul is gone
Betwixt his two breder in wilder' tho' alone.

No. 16.

"*Syne home fairst ya draw.*" This probably means—Since they like to take people home to embalm. "*Fairst*" may perhaps be for "*fainest,*" most gladly. Anthony was very anxious not to be embalmed, and on this very account had taken up his abode in the mountain. He enjoined his friends to tell nobody where they buried him, for that in the resurrection he should receive his body incorruptible from his Saviour.

Her in wildernes they bery him that no man shall hy' knaw
For so he com'anded syne home fairst ya draw.

No. 17.

It is evident that the idea of Anthony's living alone with the boar is a mistake. He lived upwards of twenty years alone; but this was before he knew the wild boar, which is evidently the beast he caressed in the garden when he was more hospitably disposed. Mrs. Jamieson says the boar is allegorical; but when the story first appeared I cannot make out.

> Thus levyth he in wildernes xx^{iv} yer & more
> Without any company but the wild boore.

The Venerable Bede, whose History of St. Cuthbert, his contemporary, is illustrated in these paintings, was born at Jarrow, in 673, and educated at Wearmouth, where he afterwards taught. He wrote Commentaries on the Holy Scriptures, an Ecclesiastical History of England, and translated the Gospel of St. John into Saxon, which he completed on the day and hour of his death, in May, 735. His relics were translated to Durham.

1

Her Cuthbert was forbid laykes & playe
As S. Bede i' hys story sayes

2

Her the angel did hym ....le
And made hym for..........

3

Her saw he Aydan .... sowl upgo
to hevyn blyss wt Angels two

4

Her to hym and hys palfray
God send hym Fude in hys Iurnay

5

Melrose

6

The Angel he did as yeat refreshe
Wt mete & drynk thys seke washe

7

Her while teld hym yt he must de
And after yt he .... shuld be

Nre to hys bredren two —— ehe
he preched godys word myld & mek

Here stude he naked in ye see
till David Psalter sayd had he

10

He was gydyd by ye egle fre
And fed wt ye delfyne an ye see

11

Her by prayers sendys obt farn glad
And wt angel hâds hout in ......

12

Fresh water god sent owt of ye ston
to hym in fer u i be for in ...... on

13

The crowes yt did his howse untheck
ye sorfull lowe fell at his fete

Conſecrate byſshop yai made hym her
off lyndisfarne both far and ner

To thys child god grace ....
through his prayers .. asyemyde

Nyȝ bysshop t Woyerys when he had beyn
in ȝarte he died both holy & cleare

xj yere after yt beryd was he.
yai fand him hole as red may ye

LEGEND OF ST. CUTHBERT.

No. 1.

St. Cuthbert, untill the age of eight years, was only delighted in all manner of childish sports and pastimes which that age is wont to follow, ever desiring to be with the first at boyish meetings and places of gaming; and being of a piercing witt, and by nature framed to agility and nimbleness, he was wont, for the most part, to gett the upper hand of all his other rivalls in leaping, running, and wrestling, or anie other such exercise; insomuch that when they were all wearied, he, like an untamed little champion and victor of them all, would merryly demand yf anie were disposed to buckle with him anie more. But being once in the fields, in the heatt of these youthful sports, it pleased the Allmightie God to touch him with a quite contrarie spirit. For a little child, but three years old as it seemed, came to him, and with an aged constancie beganne seriously to exhort him to forsake those childish exercises, and to betake himself to a more modest and grave manner of life. But he slighting those, as he thought, babish admonitions, repayd them home with injurious words, when the child fell flat on the earth, and with a pittiful countenance blubbered with tears, spake to Cuthbert, who came to comfort him, with these words—"O most holy Bishop Cuthbert, it is not seemly for thee to play the child amongst children, whom Allmightie God hath ordained and destined to be a master of virtue unto ancients." Cuthbert gave diligent care hereunto; and this speech remayned fixt in his mind, the same holie spiritt instructing him inwardly in his soule, that by the mouthe of the infant spake openly to his hearing.

Her Cuthbert was forbid layks* and plays
As Bede in his story says.

No. 2.

And to give him further warning, he was suddenly taken with such an exceeding paine and contraction in one of his knees, that by no means was he able to go. Till being carried forth one day into the fields a little to recreate his spiritts with the sight of those green carpets of nature; and reposing himself under the open heavens, he perceived a horseman, exceedingly shining in apparell, come towards him, who demanded if he would showe anie service to such a guest? "Most willingly (replied Cuthbert, and showing his knee) did not this paine hold me prisoner for faults past. For this is a grief which exceeds all art of Physick to remedie." Hereat the horseman lighted, and diligently viewing and reviewing the sore, "Boyle (said he) some wheeten flower in milk, and applie it hott to the swelling, and thou shalt be cured." This said, he ridd swiftly on his way, and at the same instant Cuthbert came to know he was an angel. And from this time the devout child (as he himself was wont to assure his familiar friends) being oftentimes beset with adversities, through his prayers to Allmightie God deserved to be guarded by an angel, and by the same means to deliver others out of the straights of many eminent dangers.

Her the angel did hym.........le
And made his sor†..................

---

* Layks, a north-country word for sport.
† [Sore]. Perhaps the rhymes may be *hele* [heal] and *weal*.

No. 3.

But it happened afterwards that he was turned to the wild mountains to become a sheepherd. Whereas one night, all his fellowes being asleep, he watched carefully over his flock, and passed over the tedious howers of the night in prayer, he beheld a glittering sight which dispersed the night's horrid shades, and a greate troupe of bright, shining creatures, which came down from heaven and carried up the soule of St. Aidan, Bishop of Lindisfarne, a man of wonderful virtue and pietie, to the joyes of everlasting happiness. Being greatly astonished and rejoyced with this vision, "If for one night's watching and prayer (said he to himself) I have deserved to behold such wonders, what reward shall I receive yf I lend all the powers of my soule wholly to the contemplation of divine things?" And at the same instant he resolved to forsake his flocks and to embrace a monasticall life.

Her saw he Ayda*.........sowl up go
To hevyns blyss w^t angels two.

No. 4.

Therefore shaking off the fetters of the world, he departed thence and entered into the way of heaven, travelling night and day alone, without eyther meate or drinke, to find out a quiet haven wherein he might securely harbour at the sweete shore of contemplation. At length he arrived at a village, where he stayed only to refresh his wearied horse; for he himself could not be entreated to taste anie food, because it was Friday, on which day

* [Aydan's soul go up to heaven's bliss.]

he fasted in honour of our Lord's passion. Thence, therefore, he departed fasting, and held on his journey through deserts and forlorn places, which he could not overcome before he was overtaken by night, so that he was constrained at length to lodge in a poore forsaken cabbin, expecting the next day-light; when, falling to his prayers as his custom was, greatly moved with compassion to see the poore beast, his horse, quite toiled and tired out with the journey, almost fainting for want of food, he gathered up a handfull of hay, which the wind had blowne off that weake cottage, and gave it him to eate; which done, againe he tooke himselfe to his prayers for the space of a long hower, when in the meane time he saw his horse lift up his head and (hunger compelling him thereunto) he began to unthatch that poore cabbin, still drawing it down by morsels, till at length there fell out a white linnen cloth wrapped up together, which the holy young man perceiving, having ended his devotions, he opened it and found therein half a hott loafe and as much meate as was sufficient for one meale. Being greatly astonished hereat, he lifted up his hands and eyes towards heaven and gave thankes unto Allmightie God. "I acknowledge, O Lord (sayd he), that it is the bòuntie of Thy goodness which hath vouchsafed to feed me in this forlorne sollitude, as in times past thou didst nourish Elias in the desert."

Her to hym and his palfray
God send him fude in his journay.

No. 5.

At length he arrived at the desired end of his journey, the Monasterie of Mailross, where at his first coming he was prophetically commended by a holy man named Boisel, who no sooner beheld Cuthbert but he cried out to the assistants—"Behold a true servant of God!" And having understood his pious decrees, he made them known unto the holy Abbot Eata, who presently gave him the Benedictine habit.

............Mellross............
....

No. 6.

After some years, King Alchfried having bestowed some land at Rippon for the building of a new monasterie, Eata made choice of Cuthbert, with other religious monks, to furnish the same, under the same rule and monasticall discipline as the other. And within a while he was put into the office of receaving and entertayning the guests and other poore pilgrims which came to the monasterie, wherein he discharged his dutie with so great joy and diligence that every one highly commended their good entertaynment and his extraordinary good will. Going forth early one morning to visit the cell of his guests, he found among the rest a young man of a very beautiful countenance, and taking him to be a man indeed, he entertayned him after his sweete manner of courtesie, gave him water for his hands, washed and dried his feete, covered the table, and let pass no dutie of his charitable office. And as he urged him to eate and repaire his forces, weakened with travelling, the guest refused. "I conjure thee by the name of Allmightie God (replied Cuthbert) to refreshe thyselfe a little, whilst I goe fetch thee a loafe bread, newly bakt." He went, and returning with all speed possible, found that his new guest was gone. Whereat being amazed, he sought in the snow newly fallen to trace which way he had gone; but finding no signe of him, he was more amazed than before; and casting his eyes aboute, he perceaved that he had left there three milk white loaves, behind him, from which came a moste sweete odour; and then, with trembling, he began to imagine that it was an angel he had entertayned, who came not to be fede, but to feede.

The angel he did as gest refreshe
W^t^ mete & drynk & his fete weshe.

No. 7.

But within a short time Eata was obliged to leave the monasterie he had built and return with Cuthbert and the rest of his monks to Mailross, where Cuthbert, holding on the pious course of his monasticall life, governed himselfe chiefly by the good counsell and admonitions of the most holie man Boisel, prior of that place. Afterwards, Boisel being dead, Cuthbert succeeded to the government of the monasterie.

Her Bosel told hym he must de [die]
And after y^t^ he........ suld be.

[*Prior*, of course, is the word to be supplied in the second verse.]

No. 8.

Which office he discharged with wonderful greate example of virtue and diligence, not onlie for the spirituall profitt of his own domestiques, but also by his fruitful endeavour in converting the common people thereabouts from the bad waies of their vices and fond customs to the love of heaven and heavenly joyes, partly by the good example of his virtuous and holie life, partly with his holie *sermons* and exhortations, and partly by the miraculous cure of many diseases.

Her to his bred[ren] & Pa[gans] eke
He preched Gods word mylde & mek.

No. 9.

In the meane time the holie man began to excell in the spirit of prophecy, to foretell things to come, and declare things absent. For being upon some important necessitie of his monasterie to take shipping, with two other monkes, to pass into the land of the Picts called Niduars, and the faire calmness of the weather putting them in hope to make a speedie returne, they went forth wholly unfurnished of provision in victuals; but it fell out otherwise; for they were no sooner on land than there rose such a blustering and tempestuous wind, that the sea, moved with these tempestuous blasts, began alsoe to be puffed up into whole mountains of outragious waves, which hindered them quite from thinking how to returne. Soe that beinge there among the cruelties of cold and hunger for the space of some dayes, they were almost all starved to death through want of victuals, when the holie man was never idle, but watching night and day in prayer, comforted his fellowes with pious discourses, invited them to fall to their prayers and commit themselves into the hands and protection of Allmightie God, who would doubtless succour them in their necessity, as he did the children of Israel in the desert. [It was not an uncommon practice with the Saints to recite the whole of the Psalter, and to stand in cold water. Cuthbert may be supposed to be praying for calm weather and for food.]

Her stude he naked in the se
Till all David's Psalter sayd had he,

No. 10.

(1) And now, sayd he, "Let us go to find what sustenance our Lord has sent us his servants." Then leading them under the bank where he had prayed a little before, they found three pieces or portions of dolphin's flesh readie to be boyled. "You see, deare brethren (sayd he), how great a grace it is to be confident in Allmyghtie God. Behold, he hath not onlie sent food to his hongrie servants, but, by the number of three, signifies how many daies we must yet remayne here before the tempest cease." And it fell out as the holie man foretold. [This is alluded to in the couplet, but not represented.]

(2) Going forth one day to preach, accompanied only with a little boy, and both being wearied with their journey and destitute of anie food to repaire their weakened forces, "Tell me, child (sayd the holie man), what courage thou hast by this time, seeing that we have neither meate nor drinke to satisfie our hunger, nor noe place whither to retire ourselves for shelter." "That is it (replied he) which greatly troubles me, since we have neither victuals, nor money to buy, nor friend to assist us." "Be comforted, my child, in the goodness of Allmightie God (answered Cuthbert), and rest assured he will never abandon those in time of necessitie who give themselves faythfullie and with all their hearts to his divine service. Doest thou see that eagle yonder which flies in the ayre? mark her well; for by her means our Lord will send us succour in this extremetie." With such like discourse they held on their journey by the river side, when the eagle, having taken a fishe, laid it for them on the banke. The one half the holie man caused to be left for their divine purveyor,

and with the remaynder he refreshed himselfe and his companion in the next village."

He was gydyd by the Egle fre
And fed with the delfyne as ye se.

No. 11 (13* in the series).

Eata sends Cuthbert from Mailross to Lindisfarne, whence he obtains leave to go, after some years, to the island Farnen "to enjoye the sweete loneliness of a long desired solitude and divine contemplation."

He departed, therefore, to the island Farnen, soe infamous by the habitation and infection of devilish spiritts, that none durst ever before dwell there alone; but this ice, our holy Cuthbert brake, when, like a worthy champion, armed with the helmet of health, the buckler of fayth, and the sword of the Spyritt, which is the Word of God, he opposed himself against that hellish crewe, and dissipated, dissolved, and put to flight all their infernal troupes.

Her by prayers Fendys out farn glad
And with angels hands hys house he made.

[There is nothing to illustrate the last line in the history (see note). The first line means that he drove the fiends from Farnen (or the Fern) Islands, where there are great numbers of sea birds. "Out farn" probably is "*out faren,*" go out; unless "farn" means Farnen Islands. "*Glad*" signifies "*easily*" in north-country dialect.]

NOTE.—The waves of the sea did serve him when they cast upon the land a piece of *timber* just the *length* he *desired*.

No. 12 (11 in the series).

But his habitation being quite destitute of water (following another miracle of our great Father, St. Benedict),

* The Nos. 13, 11, 16, 12, 14, 15, in the series on the back of the stalls, which are here distinguished by the parenthesis, differ in the order as given in Bede's History.

he obtayned by his prayers to Allmyghtie God to have a sweete chrystall fountaine spring out of the hard rock.

Fresh water God sent out of the ston
To him in Farn & before [was n]on.

No. 13 (16 in the series).

He lived by the labour of his hands, digging and tilling the earth, and sowing it first with wheat, which brethren brought hym. But that his weake land would not bring to good; therefore he sowed it with barley, which increased in great abundance, when the byrds, that in great troupes sought to devour his litle harvest, were forced at his only command to depart and never more touch his corne. The like he commanded and was obeyed by the crowes and dawes, which laboured to teare off the thatch of his humble dwelling. But one of them returning again to the holy man, lamentably spreading her wings abrode, bowing down her head, and making a pitifull noise, seemed by all signes possible to entreate pardon, which the holy man understanding, gave her leave to returne, as presently she did, bringing a mate with her, and for a present to the saint, the one half of a hogges grease, which the holy man was wont oftentimes to show to the monks his brethren and give them part of it to liquor their shoes or bootes. See heere againe the spiritt of his greate master St. Benedict in the obedience and service of the crowes.

The crowys y[t] did his hous unthek*
y[s] for full law fell at his fete.†

* Unthatch. † This for full low fell at his feet.

No. 14 (12 in the series).

But a council being held at Adtwiford, under St. Theodore, Archbishop of Canterbury, in the presence of King Egfried, by the common presented desire of all, Cuthbert was chosen Bishop of Lindisfarne, who being by many letters and legates sent from the king and councill called to the sinod to reseave that charge, he would not stir a foote; for unworthy that was most worthy judged he himself of that dignitie. At length good King Egfried himself, with the most holy Bishop Trumaine, and manie other religious and noble persons, went over into the island, and falling upon their knees before the holy man, with teares and humble entreaties, they besought and conjured him by the name of the Lord not to resist the wishes and desires of soe manie and to oppose himself to the common good of the Church. Neither did they cease untill Cuthbert, as full of teares and sorrow as an honest heart could be, suffered himself to be drawn out of his beloved cell of solitariness and drawn into the councill, where, being vehemently urged of all, he was compelled, much against his will, to yield to their desires. In the Easter following he was consecrated Bishop of Lindisfarne, in presence of the King, blessed Theodore of Canterbury, and seven other Bishops of Yorke.

Consecrate Byshop yai made by' her
Of Lyndisfarne both far & nere.

[From the time of Constantine it was thought proper, if not incumbent, on those who were consecrated Priests or Bishops, to decline in the first instance.]

No. 15 (14 in the series).

He cured a child dying of the plague by giving him a kisse and making the sign of the crosse upon him.

To this child God grace............
Thro hys prayers as ye may se.

No. 16 (15 in the series).

When he had been Byshop two yeares he resigned his pastoral office, and retired to Farne Island to die, but consented to be buried at Lindisfarne. Having armed himself with the sacred viaticum of our Lord's bodie, lifting up his hands and eyes to heaven, he yielded up his blessed soule to the everlasting joies of heaven.

> Byshop two yeares when he had beyn
> Lyndisfarne he died both holy & clene.

No. 17.

Eleven yeares after his decease, upon some occasion, the monks would needs take up his sacred bones (imagining the flesh to be turned to that it came of) to set them in a more eminent place or monument above ground. Whereunto holy Eadbert verie willinglie consented, and caused his sepulchre to be opened on the verie day of his deposition; when, to the greate admiration of all, they found his bodie whole and without the least blemish, his joints pliant and flexible as if he had been alive, and, in a word, more like a man asleepe than to one that were dead. Likewise all the vestments about him were not onlie entire and sound, but shining as pich, and new as when they were made.

> xi yeare after beryed was he
> Yai found hym hole as red [read] may ye.

"CALENDAR OF THE ANGLICAN CHURCH," p. 339.

The series of the twelve Apostles is frequently met with in church decoration, as on the west fronts of Wells and Exeter Cathedrals, and many other churches in Norfolk and Suffolk. They are usually to be distinguished, when thus grouped together, by the same emblems as in the individual representations, except that St. John generally appears in his character of an apostle with the chalice and snake, and not as an Evangelist with the eagle; and St. Matthew with the purse or carpenter's square, and not with the angel. In many instances they have each a scroll containing a sentence from the Creed, in accordance with the tradition that before they separated after the ascension, they met for the purpose of deciding upon a confession of faith, and that each furnished one article of belief, the whole being comprehended in what is now termed the Apostles' Creed. These are assigned as follows:—

They do not invariably consist of the same twelve, Matthias, Jude, and St. James the less, being occasionally omitted; and Paul, Mark, Luke, (rarely John the Baptist), *Thaddeus, as in Carlisle Cathedral, being inserted in their

* Jude.

places. The Saviour frequently occupies the centre compartment.

Credo in Deum Patrem Omnipotentem Creatorem Cœli et Terræ	Petrus
Et in Ihm Xpm filium ejus unicum Dominum nostrum	Andras
Qui conceptus est de Spiritu Sancto natus ex Maria Virgine	Jacobus
Passus est sub Pontio Pilato, Crucifixus Mortuus et Sepultus	Johannes
Descendit ad inferos, tertia die resurrexit e Mortuis	Thomas
Ascendit ad cœlos, sedet ad dextram Dei Patris Omnipotentis	Jacobus
Inde venturus est judicare vivos et mortuos	Philippus
Credo in Spiritum Sanctum	Bartholomieu
Sanctor^{m} communionem	Matthew
Remissionem Peccatorum	Simon
Carnis resurrectionem	Thaddeus
Et Vitam Eternam	Matthias

dominum nostrum

Qui conceptus est de Spiritu Sancto
Natus est Maria Virgine. Jacobus
Passus est sub poncio pelato crucifixus
Mortuus et sepultus. Johannes

Descendit ad infer.... tertio die
resurrexit a mortuis Thomas
Ascendit ad Caelos sedit ad dextram
dei patris omnipotentis. Jacobus

Inde venturus est iudicare
vivos et mortuos
Philippus
Credo in Spiritum Sanctum.
Bartholo-

Scam ecclesiam catholicam
Sanctorm communionem. Matheus
Remissionem peccatorum
Simon

Carnis resurrectionem
Thaddeus
Et vitam aeternam
Mathias

www.ingramcontent.com/pod-product-compliance
Lightning Source LLC
Chambersburg PA
CBHW030851270326
41928CB00008B/1321
* 9 7 8 3 7 4 1 1 5 8 1 9 3 *